How to Stop Project 2025

A guide to legally stop the Far Right in Trump's regime and protect U.S. human rights

By Diane Lilli

Rebel Books Press
RebelBooksPress.com

First published in the United States of America
by Rebel Books Press November 2024

Copyright © November 2024 by Diane Lilli

How to Stop Project 2025
A guide to stop the Far Right in Trump's regime
and protect U.S. human rights

All Rights Reserved
This book is a work of nonfiction.

Paperback ISBN 979-8-3305-6121-6
eBook ISBN 979-8-3305-6122-3
First Edition

Printed in the United States of America
For information about special discounts for bulk purchases, please
email Editor@rebelpressbooks.com for bulk orders

Available wherever books are sold.

This book is dedicated to the humanists who will fight legally to protect the U.S. Constitution and safeguard human rights in the United States of America, and to our loved ones who may have lost their way. We miss you and we love you.

How to Use This Book

This book was completed on November 15, 2024. I did not want to write this book, but as an author and American citizen, I knew it was my duty to do try to help others, in any way possible, to protect our Democracy, even in a small way.

My sleepless nights began in June 2024, as I feared that the far-right, under the influence of Project 2025, would win the election with Donald Trump.

The steady march of the far-right conservative agenda under incoming President Donald Trump offers many frightening, unconstitutional policies that they have promised will become law.

Will our country fall? We are living in very dark times, and I do not know. Project 2025 is the backbone of the incoming President's vision and administration. This is my plan to help us get organized.

How to use this guide

1. Choose a cause.

2. Read the facts about that cause, in that section.

3. Choose one of the nonprofit US organizations you can contact to get information for local and national participation.

If you need any help, please email us at editor@rebelbookspress.com

Connecting Dots between Project 2025 and Donald Trump

How to End Project 2025 is a guide that I hope will help change the course of our threatened Democracy. I have included my name as author, though I understand that President Donald Trump was serious when he said numerous times he would retaliate against the free press.

"I say up front, openly, and proudly, that when I WIN the Presidency of the United States, they and others of the Lame Stream Media will be thoroughly scrutinized for their knowingly dishonest and corrupt coverage of people, things, and events," Trump said in a public campaign rally in September 2024, saying that the press "should pay a big price" for allegedly hurting the country.

As the First Amendment of the Constitution clearly states, "Congress shall make no law respecting an establishment of religion or prohibiting the free exercise thereof; or abridging the freedom of speech, or of the press; or the right of the people peaceably to assemble, and to petition the Government for a redress of grievances."

This book is a call to action. I kept it simple, with facts, information about each Constitutional and/or human rights violations that we may face, and included powerful nonprofit organizations that will help every issue.

Use this book as a guide for information and ideas on how to overturn policies of the far-right nationalists, the 47th president of the United States takes office.

Simultaneously, please remember that this was a legal election and Trump won, fair and square. About 74,650,754 American voters (as of November 10, 2024) voted for Donald Trump and support his vision for the future of our country.

Please do not waste time and fall into a rabbit hole of conspiracy lunacy, as Trump followers did when he lost the election to President Joe Biden in 2020. We have no time to waste. We are all on call to step out of the massive shadow of grief and immediately do the hard work and commit to make change in our country; by protecting our Constitutional rights and all human rights violations headed our way by our own government.

My goal is to help you understand the issues and then take simple steps to fight the barrage of human rights violations we expect will begin on Inauguration Day, January 20, 2025, and beyond.

Using live and taped videos from Trump's campaign rallies; podcasts; TV appearances on Fox News and all newspapers, plus the presidential debates, How to End Project 2025 uses the public promises of President Trump, that he clearly said will become a reality in 2025. As we go to press now, on November 15, President- elect Donald Trump is naming his cabinet members and heads of American agencies. It is shocking.

It is impossible not to see the obvious influence the far-right Project 2025 propaganda has had upon our incoming president, and that his administration will most likely disrupt our American Democracy in frightening ways.

Make no mistake: we are in great danger of losing many of our precious human rights, with the nationalist, far-right new Republicans (not all Republicans but most) leading the way.

I see a lust for power by the current Republican leaders and many members that ignore what really makes our country powerful and beautiful: our Founding Father's mission that all men (and women) are created equal. Even our right to keep religion and church separate are being threatened.

Non-violence can work for change, and I believe that everyday Americans and others who work in their local communities can join local plus national new types of protests, in person or in a unique social media outreach. Many of these battles will begin in grassroots protests, and local plus national lawsuits.

We must also rely upon our youngest generations to lead the way in a full-scale social media battle, from TikTok to Instagram and all platforms, including Facebook for the older generations.

Social media helped us get into this mess so we need to use it brilliantly, right now. Our clear agenda is to protect Democracy, but also inform many of our loved ones, who believe that our incoming Trump administration is not a threat to our citizens, of what is happening in government.

Only time will tell, but I am fearful, as are millions of Americans, global citizens and leaders across the globe, that our almost 250 years as a true Democracy will be damaged, perhaps beyond repair.

Why do I believe this? I have listened to the promises and slurs used in the presidential election, and it is obvious to me that our divided country is going to experience some mighty changes.

What you will read are the disturbing recommendations made in Project 2025, some of which became part of the national conversation and rants during Trump rallies. I am sure you've all seen and heard them. Now, Trump is organizing his cabinet and heads of government agencies, with only "loyal" supporters, most of whom have very little or no experience in government. Do they understand the Constitution? If not, they can read the last page of this book, where I included it.

I urge you to use this guide and craft a unique, nonviolent revolution that is lawful, respectful, and loud. Do not be afraid to work legally to fight the expected violation of civil rights we will face in 2025 and beyond. Protest! Work with these organizations, and start your own if you can, to protect our most vulnerable citizens.

Is there a possibility that conditions will change so drastically that we will lose our legal right to protest? Will we experience an ending to safe protests and freedom of speech? Yes, and if so, we must pivot somehow. We cannot predict how things will go, so for now, we must prepare to calmly choose a cause listed here (and any new ones that pop up) and work with others in your own community, and on a national level, to save our Constitutional rights.

At the time of this book's publication, I can assure you we will need to constantly keep on top of human rights violations. And, we need to free the millions of frightened Americans who fell victim to what I believe is a cult of personality and rage.

However, we cannot remain a divided nation, if we are to survive. Though we will work hard to end Project 2025 and Trump's far right dismantling of numerous agencies, we must also remember that many of our loved ones believe that everything will be fine, and that we are catastrophizing the upcoming Trump Administration.

This is no time to cancel your close relationships with loved ones who voted for Trump. Instead, share this book, and help show them why millions of Americans are scared to death that our Democracy will die. Open up a line of communication and do not use anger.

Beyond the tsunami of daily offensive new polices coming our way, we must remember that somehow, we must create a way to end our national divide and accept each other, with a caveat that we can ONLY do this if we support the rights of ALL people. Do NOT give up in fear, if the worst happens. I cannot predict what we can do if our Constitutional Democracy fails under the chaos of never-ending attacks with new executive orders that ignore the rule of law. I do expect this will happen, but I can't understand how we can overturn such chaos peacefully – that is where I am stuck. If our system fails us, what can we do? I have no answers yet. For now, this is my small attempt to help you be ready for the biggest fight of our lives: to protect our Constitution.

What is Project 2025 and how will it harm or end our Democracy?

Project 2025 is a 900-page manual written by former Trump officials, in an alliance with The Heritage Foundation, a far-right think tank that opposes LGBTQ rights, immigrants' rights, abortion and reproductive rights, racial equality, and much more.

Their "Mandate for Leadership" calls for all Federal Government Agencies to be dismantled and reorganized as conservative agendas, and in the manual, it clearly describes Draconian far-right, extreme religious inspired guidelines.

How is President Donald Trump connected to Project 2025?

Trump denies his connection or allegiance to Project 2025, but his during his campaign he shouted his polices, matching plenty of Project 2025 mandates to his followers. He denies following or knowing much about the manual, but CNN reported that about 140 people who worked on the manual also worked for Donald Trump in his administration.[1]

The Heritage Foundation President Kevin Roberts, in an article in the New York Times, described his organization's impact upon Trump as "Institutionalizing Trumpism." [2] You may remember Mr. Roberts as the leading voice that called for overturning the 2020 presidential election, and to keep then-President Donald Trump in office, even though there was never any proof this "steal the vote" occurred.

---

[1] https://www.cnn.com/2024/07/11/politics/trump-allies-project-2025/index.html
[2] https://www.nytimes.com/2024/01/21/magazine/heritage-foundation-kevin-roberts.html

Connect the dots: Trump campaigned using much of Project 2025's neo-nationalist guide taken right out of the Project 2025 playbook. Trump's master plan for a radical, Project 2025 inspired overhaul of the US government is real.

As of today, here is a list of top issues to fight. Newly elected President Trump is already creating policies and new initiatives that are aligned with Project 2025.

Once Trump is in office, I expect total chaos and a slew of executive orders that attack our Constitution. Will the courts prevail? I fear they will not, but hope they will surprise us.

4. Choose a cause.
5. Read the facts about that cause, in that section.
6. Choose one of the nonprofit US organizations you can contact to get information for local and national participation.

If you need any help, please email us at projectforever2025@gmail.com

Undocumented Immigrants are Under Fire As Nationalism takes over our government

"Remember, remember always, that all of us, you and I especially, are descended from immigrants and revolutionists."

Franklin D. Roosevelt

The facts of undocumented immigrants in the U.S. and what President Trump promised to do once elected

It is not legal to enter this country or any country illegally. But it certainly happens.

Most immigrants flee their homes under threat of death, religious prosecution, or economic disasters. Soon, a new type of immigrant, the 'climate refugee' will become the largest type of immigrants worldwide. However, there are also violent actors crossing our borders.

In the US, immigrants can arrive legally and apply for US citizenship, which is not easy to obtain. One of the main reasons immigrants are accepted in the U.S. is that they are under threat of death in their home country.

Pew Research reports that the "unauthorized immigrant population in the United States grew to 11.0 million in 2022" and that in 2007 it was much higher, at 12.2 million."[3]

If you have watched or listened to Donald Trump during his presidential campaign, he used numerous inflated totals for the numbers of illegal immigrants in the U.S., none of which are real.

---

[3] https://www.pewresearch.org/short-reads/2024/07/22/what-we-know-about-unauthorized-immigrants-living-in-the-us/

He also repeatedly said that immigrants are violent criminals, are voting illegally, eating your pets (especially in Springfield!), using up emergency disaster funding and stealing American jobs.

Fact checks

How many illegal immigrants are violent criminals?

Donald Trump claimed on Trump social that *"13,000 convicted murderers"* entered the U.S. under Biden."[4] This is untrue. Those numbers of murderers are from ANYONE ANYTIME that entered our borders illegally, so it goes back years. Are there violent undocumented immigrants in our country? Of course there are, and they need to be deported.

How many illegal immigrants are voting illegally? Again, Trump used disinformation during his campaign. Our voting systems are secure, and it is nearly impossible to vote illegally. This disinformation fuels all kinds of extremist groups, who want to replace our population, much like Nazis did, with mostly white people. It is also part of the Project 2025 agenda.

Are illegal Immigrants depleting our Emergency Disaster funds? No. FEMA officials said they can meet their immediate needs for disaster funds but back-to-back hurricanes and tornadoes, wildfires, and flooding mean they may need to request more aid from Congress.

Do illegal immigrants eat our pets (especially in Springfield, Ohio? Of course not – ask the mayor of Springfield (which I did).

Are illegal immigrants stealing our jobs?

No, absolutely not. As a matter of fact, data on U.S. employment reports that undocumented immigrants are mostly filling the vacant jobs that Americans refuse to take. Furthermore, these undocumented workers pay taxes, so they are helping our

---

[4] https://www.latimes.com/politics/story/2024-10-31/we-fact-checked-some-of-trumps-most-common-claims-on-immigration

economy with millions of tax dollars paid! Two out of three undocumented immigrants make up our farm workers, and the construction industry is already warning that if we kick out all their immigrants, we will have housing crisis. [5]

Incumbent President Donald Trump has vowed to being removing illegal immigrants from the U.S. on "day one."

Noone is advocating for opening orders and letting immigrants just enter the U.S. of course. We have a system and if it's broken, let's fix it in a humane way.

What Trump promised to do with undocumented immigrants when he takes office.

They will conduct mass deportations. His plans include sweeps across the U.S. (probably by the National Guard) to find and take illegal immigrants away.

He has said, repeatedly, that he will build detention camps.

They will conduct raids.

In the new Trump administration, we expect he will end birthright citizenship, which is for anyone born in the U.S. who is a child of an illegal immigrant.

Trump will close southern borders.

Trump is also expected to dismantle our asylum system, which protects people in great danger in their native country.

As of today, due to Trump's numerous appointments of "loyalists", including his longtime advisor Stephen Miller, who will serve as his deputy chief of staff for policy. Some of his polices include separating migrant children from their families, and the plan for mass deportation of the undocumented immigrants.

Mr. Miller also published a post on X after the election saying that he will "turbocharge" immigration deportations.

In a statement, the Nonprofit Organization Hub said,

---

[5] https://www.latimes.com/politics/story/2024-10-31/we-fact-checked-some-of-trumps-most-common-claims-on-immigration

"Their Project 2025 agenda would target naturalized citizens and see those who have earned their place in this country deported. The denaturalization campaign that began under Trump, and which close advisor Stephen Miller now promises to "turbocharge" is an attack on the fundamental principles of fairness, stability, and equal rights that citizenship represents. Such policies are rooted in fear and exclusion, not in the principles of justice and equality that should guide our nation." [6]

---

[6] https://theimmigrationhub.org/press/gop-plans-to-turbocharge-trumps-denaturalization-project-threaten-the-nations-core-values/

Immigration Nonprofit Resources

Immigration Hub
The Immigration Hub is a national organization committed to winning protections for millions of aspiring citizens by leading innovative advocacy campaigns, generating powerful narrative interventions and forging groundbreaking alliances.
https://theimmigrationhub.org/

Immigration Advocates Network
This organization is a free national online network that supports legal advocates working on behalf of immigrants' rights.
https://www.immigrationadvocates.org/nonprofit/legaldirectory/

USCRI
We provide legal, social, and health services to refugees, unaccompanied migrating children, trafficking survivors, and other immigrants in all 50 states.
https://refugees.org/

United Farm Workers of America
THE UFWA fights for the rights of farm workers, Mexican American immigrants, women, and LGBTQ population
https://ufw.org/

Dismantling the Department of Education Removing LBGTQI rights Preventing Trans students' medical care
Deleting civil rights for students

The war against the LBGTQI community is ramping up to be extremely anti-Trans students and most likely gay students under Trump's newly formed cabinet, who has the power to make stark changes. The Department of Education is a cabinet organization since 1980.

As you may know, during his campaign, Trump said he will "dismantle" the Department of Education. Congress must allow this action, but remember: Trump can gut the department first, and ask for ending it later. This is my greatest fear.

Now, the Trump administration is gearing up to destroy the Department of Education and recreate a new agency. Trump said they will cut federal funding for schools teaching critical race theory, bar transgender female athletes from participating in school sports, and stop all critical race theory education.

Furthermore, the new Trump presidency is expected to weaponize federal law in numerous ways so both states and citizens can sue schools that offer protection to Trans students' rights, or event protests on campus. They also can use federal law to legally stop hospitals for providing gender-affirming medical care to trans adolescents. (Expect the DOJ to be gutted.)

Once the Department of Education is dismantled, the Office of Civil Rights, which enforces the federal civil rights laws in American schools and protect all students against discrimination will disappear, because it exists inside the Department of Education.

Clearly, LBGTQI rights and education plus civil rights for students, are connected in the dismantling of The Department of Education by Trump.

During his campaign, Trump promised to "cut federal funding for any school or program pushing Critical Race Theory or gender ideology on our children." Critical Race Theory is taught in schools to educate students about systemic racism that is deeply embedded in American society.

With the dismantling of the Department of Education, the Trump team can then change federal laws for schools, so LBGTQI students and gay students are not protected. In addition, since the Department of Education designates all federal aid via Title I, for state and local school funding serving low-income families, these services are now in great jeopardy.

The ACLU reports that "over 100 state laws attacking transgender people and their rights have passed since 2020." As of 2024, they add, "23 states have laws explicitly protecting LGBTQ people from discrimination at work, in school, and in public spaces."[7]

The new Trump administration plans to dismantle the Department of Education to control the curriculums in our schools. This is an effort to stifle the rights of all students, including LBGTQI and anyone with a different point of view than the Project 2025 followers.

Whoever controls education controls tomorrow's generation. Of all the battles we must face, this may be the most urgent one.

Just look at Florida's Draconian "Don't Say Gay' laws that were recently expanded.

1. Florida bans classroom instruction on gender identity and sexual orientation to all grades.

---

[7] https://www.aclu.org/issues/lgbtq-rights

2. Under the Parental Rights Law, signed into law 2022, at first teachers were prohibited to do any instruction on gender identity and sexual orientation is banned for K-3 students.
3. Now, all public-school students will be banned from learning about these topics, unless required by existing state standards or as part of reproductive health instruction that students can opt out of.
4. Florida prohibits sexual orientation or gender identity instruction in prekindergarten through eighth grade, restricts reproductive health education in sixth through 12th grade and requires that reproductive health instruction "be age-appropriate or developmentally appropriate for students in accordance with state standards." The law applies to both public and charter schools.

In a confusing legal settlement between Florida education officials and civil rights attorneys in March, teachers are allowed to discuss sexual orientation and gender identity in classrooms but they are prohibited from including information as part of their instruction. Does that make any sense? No.

Other states using laws similar to Florida include Alabama, Arkansas, Indiana, Iowa, Kentucky and North Carolina.

If the new Trump/Project 2025 administration gets their way, expect the US. Tourist industry to fall apart. Who can enter a country where you can only be male or female? Globally, passports do not force anyone to choose a birth sex, but instead, leave each citizen the right to say which gender they are, and leave it at that. In our dystopian US future, you will see this is a major issue and believe me: our tourism – worth $155 annually – will send our economy spinning.

LBGTQI Rights and Education Resources

GLAAD

As a dynamic media force, GLAAD ensures fair, accurate, and inclusive representation that rewrites the script for LGBTQ acceptance. GLAAD tackles tough issues to shape the narrative and provoke dialogue that leads to cultural change. GLAAD protects all that has been accomplished and envisions a world with 100% LGBTQ acceptance.

GLAAD Resource List by category
https://glaad.org/resourcelist/

Transgender Law Center

Transgender Legal Defense & Education Fund
The largest transgender organization in the U.S., advocating self-determination for all people
https://transgenderlawcenter.org/

American Civil Liberties (ACLU)

The ACLU works to ensure that lesbian, gay, bisexual, transgender and queer people can live openly without discrimination and enjoy equal rights, personal autonomy, and freedom of expression and association.

https://www.aclu.org/issues/lgbtq-rights

LAMBDA Legal

Lambda Legal's lawyers have won precedent-setting civil rights cases on everything from marriage equality to expressions of gender identity to health care discrimination. We have made legal history since day one, winning our right to incorporate. We then got to work using our knowledge of the law to fight for our community's lives and dignity.

https://lambdalegal.org/

Department of Education Resources

National Education Association (NEA)

The National Education Association (NEA) is more than 3 million people—educators, students, activists, workers, parents, neighbors, friends—who believe in opportunity for all students and in the power of public education to transform lives and create a more just and inclusive society.

https://www.nea.org/

NATIONAL CENTER FOR YOUTH LAW/ECRA

The ECRA ensures the civil rights of historically and presently marginalized students are protected by providing resources to students, parents, educators, school districts, and advocates on creating safe, inclusive, and affirming schools, supporting state and local legal enforcement actions when school districts and states fail to do so, raising public awareness of the challenges students face, and serving as a deterrent to discriminatory school policies and practices.

https://youthlaw.org/

Abortion Laws may lead to Federal ban
Abortion meds may become illegal

In the 2024 presidential election, seven states won abortion rights. However, the new Donald Trump presidency will make these 'wins' vulnerable, because of Project 2025's anti-abortion stance popular among far-right conservatives.

Access to abortion is unequal among states, and the new loyalists that Trump has chosen to surround him are uber-conservative. His advisers may encourage him to avoid Congress and use his federal powers to ban abortion on a national level.

Some of the Trump advisors may use the Food and Drug Administration to revoke the abortion drug mifepristone. Some of his advisors have already suggested he can use an 1800's law called the Comstock Act, that outlaws anything mailed "designed, adapted, or intended for producing abortion."

Although Trump did say states should create their own laws regarding abortion, it would not be surprising if he changes his mind. Trump's "loyalist" appointees to heads of agencies such as The Department of Justice can use the Comstock act against the manufacturers of abortion pills. Another way he can approve this is by appointing someone in his cabinet to gut abortion laws, perhaps by saying the scientifically safe abortion meds are not safe.

Wendy Parmet, director of the Center for Health Policy and Law at Northeastern University in Boston, said in an article that, "All it takes is one person in the DOJ or some zealous U.S. attorney to threaten a clinic with criminal sanction under the Comstock Act, and that could potentially cause a tremendous chill among health care providers that are providing abortion."

In 2023, the Guttmacher Institute, a major research organization that supports access to abortions, reported that there were 1,026,700 abortions in 2023.

In 1970, over 200,000 known illegal abortions were conducted in the United States, with a reported 5000 dying from botched abortions. However, since abortions were legal before Roe V Wade passed in 1973, the number of deaths by botched, secret abortions are believed to be much higher.

It's time to bring back Federal abortion rights, but at this time, we are going to busy just keeping our legal rights per state safe, because new laws under Trump may pop up to overturn them.

Abortion Rights Organizations

Planned Parenthood

Planned Parenthood has a mission to ensure all people have access to the care and resources they need to make informed decisions about their bodies, their lives, and their futures." Founded in 1916, Planned Parenthood is a trusted health care provider, educator, and passionate advocate here in the United States as well as a strong partner to health and human rights organizations around the world. Each year, Planned Parenthood delivers vital sexual and reproductive health care, sex education, and information to millions of people.

https://www.plannedparenthood.org/

Reproductive Freedom for All (NARAL)

NARAL has 2.5 million members that fight for reproductive freedom for people across the nation. Members organize to protect these freedoms by fighting for access to abortion care, birth control, paid parental leave, and protections from pregnancy discrimination. This organization leverages member-driven campaigns to inspire political and cultural change.

https://reproductivefreedomforall.org/

National Abortion Federation (NAF)

The mission of the National Abortion Federation is to unite, represent, serve, and support abortion providers in delivering patient-centered, evidence-based care.

https://prochoice.org/about/mission-leadership/

American Civil Liberties (ACLU)

The ACLU works to ensure that lesbian, gay, bisexual, transgender and queer people can live openly without discrimination and enjoy equal rights, personal autonomy, and freedom of expression and association.

https://www.aclu.org/issues/lgbtq-rights

With all-powerful Immunity The Supreme Court Made our Presidents Kings

The right to protest, freedom of speech, and protecting the free press are in grave danger. How can anyone feel safe protesting or writing an article critical of the President when the Supreme Court decided that presidents can do ....whatever they want! The Justices granted presidents broad immunity from criminal prosecution for official actions taken in office.

Time and time again in campaign rallies or television, podcast and social media posts, has promised to seek vengeance against is political enemies. He often vowed to go after his enemies in speeches at his rallies and at campaign interviews.

His angry rhetoric is not only offensive but dangerous. He said his opponents are "the enemy from within."

He loudly vowed to instruct the US Department of Justice to prosecute President Joe Biden, and members of Congress that opposed his plans for America.

Even worse, he said he invoke the Insurrection Act, a legal act that allows him to deploy the military and the National Guard against citizens who exercise their Constitutional right to protest.

Trump also said he may legally go after journalists, which is another violation of the First Amendment.

Using federal law enforcement to stop protestors and journalists is a direct act that is currently illegal in The United States of America.

But the Supreme Court, who has a powerful Conservative majority of Justices placed on the highest court by Trump, already has shocked the world with new decisions. These rulings would allow Trump, or any president, to do anything they like without breaking any laws.

Is the right to protest in danger? Yes.

Is Freedom of Speech in danger? Yes.

If Trump wants to prosecute or go after journalists, can he? Yes, if you consider there will be NO. consequences due to the new Supreme Court decision.

Can Trump retaliate against his political opponents aka anyone who does not agree with his far-right agenda? Yes, since the Supreme Court just paved the way for it.

So what if the insurrection Act is invoked? That is the scenario you must consider, sadly. Read the last section in this book, "Martial Law."

How The Supreme Court allows Presidents to do … anything

The Supreme Court has a supermajority of Republican, conservative justices appointed by Trump during his first term. In the case Trump v. U.S, the Justices created laws that make U.S. Presidents like Kings and not elected leaders.

In their decision, the Justices said that "A former president is entitled to absolute immunity from criminal prosecution for actions within his 'conclusive and preclusive constitutional authority," and "There is no immunity for unofficial acts."

The highest court in the land also added, "In dividing official from unofficial conduct, courts may not inquire into the President's motives." This means that as long as a President only plans his acts with other government staff, such as all the new loyalists about to surround our 47th president, he is immune to crime.

Got it? Donald Trump and any president, due to this insane ruling, can do whatever he likes, and no one can prosecute him – as long as he conspires with his government staff so it's an "official" act.

Supreme Court Justice Sonia Sotomayor dissented against this decision. However, she was in the minority. "Under [the majority's] rule, any use of official power for any purpose, even the most corrupt purpose indicated by objective evidence of the most corrupt motives and intent, remains official and immune," wrote Justice Sotomayor in her dissent. "Under the majority's test, if it can be called a test, the category of Presidential action that can be deemed 'unofficial' is destined to be vanishingly small." she wrote.

So can a sitting president, such as Donald Trump, assassinate his enemies?

Justice Sotomayor said, "A hypothetical President who admits to having ordered the assassinations of his political rivals or critics . . . has a fair shot at getting immunity under the majority's new Presidential accountability model."

This is an issue we must all tackle.

Supreme Court and Presidential Resources

This major issue is radically new to the U.S. it was unthinkable, until this year as the conservative super-majority in the Supreme Court, created by Trump during his first presidency, shocked the world with the new immunity decision. How can we change this?

When Congress disagrees with the Supreme Court about an interpretation of the Constitution, the only direct way to override that interpretation is for two-thirds of both houses of Congress to propose an amendment to the Constitution, which then must be ratified by three-quarters of the states

We need to change Congress. Currently, Republicans are standing meekly under Trump, as they rule both the Senate and the House.

Work on your local midterms to overturn Republicans in congress. For now, your ONLY choice is to work with Democratic party, unless you can find local Republicans who believe their party must change to protect the Constitutional rights of all.

But please remember: our votes may not count if things go wrong during the next Presidency. If the rule of law is violated, what can we do? Some experts predict civil war or worse. Let's hope we can keep our courts in order and avoid any extreme actions. Only time will tell. As a pacifist, I hope and pray this is the case, but I have no idea.

Amnesty International (USA)

Amnesty International is a global movement of millions of people demanding human rights for all people – no matter who they are or where they are.
We are the world's oldest and largest grassroots human rights organization. Since 1961, ordinary people across the world have chosen to take extraordinary action in defense of human rights for all.

https://www.amnestyusa.org/press-releases/amnesty-international-will-defend-human-rights-during-president-elect-trumps-second-term/

American Civil Liberties (ACLU)

The ACLU works to ensure that lesbian, gay, bisexual, transgender and queer people can live openly without discrimination and enjoy equal rights, personal autonomy, and freedom of expression and association.

https://www.aclu.org/issues/lgbtq-rights

Racism and Injustice under Far-right agenda

Racism is still business as usual in the U.S. especially under the far-right agenda. Incumbent President Trump is a repeated sex offender and has been convicted on 34 counts of falsifying business records to conceal payments made to the pornographic film actress Stormy Daniels, with hush money to buy her silence, over a sexual encounter between them. And who can forget the violent mob that tried to overturn the legal 2020 election, when Trump lost?

Beyond all of our incoming President's lack of civility and convictions, there is a legitimate fear the many of his voters are white Americans who support the Nazi-inspired 'great replacement theory' aka Racism.

84% of Americans who voted for Trump for president were White.

It would take ten books to document the ongoing racist problems in America. In his recent Time magazine interview, Trump said that he is going to work on what he describes as a major problem against the "definite anti-white feeling" in America. "I think there is a definite anti-white feeling in this country and that can't be allowed either," Trump said in the interview. Then he added in his comments, "But if you look right now, there's absolutely a bias against white [people] and that's a problem."

Project 2025 agrees with his sentiments. Project 2025 calls for the next Republican administration, which is happening now, to repopulate the FBI and, and have incoming President Trump run it. Trump has been naming his new often shocking department heads daily, with new choice for FBI director Kash Patel, who was an aide to Trump during his first presidency, and John Ratcliffe as the head of CIA.

Remember: he denies being involved with Project 2025 but again, he is siding with the 900-page book, of which his own vice-president Vance wrote the loving forward!

If Kash or Ratcliffe, Trump loyalists, follow the agenda of Project 2025, this logically leads to the idea that they may ignore white nationalism.

My prediction is that racism and violence against anyone who is NOT white will be an even more deadly, serious issue for the next four years.

Discrimination Resources

NAACP

Project 2025 threatens to reverse decades of progress in civil rights, social justice, and equity, impacting Black and marginalized communities. We must fight; we must advocate - we must vote - to ensure that vision does not become Our 2025.

Each and every NAACP member makes a difference to the complex, ongoing work of advancing racial equity. We have driven the hardest-fought wins for civil rights and social justice with you by our side, we can accelerate the next milestones for Black Americans.

https://naacp.org/

Amnesty International (USA)

Amnesty International is a global movement of millions of people demanding human rights for all people – no matter who they are or where they are.

We are the world's oldest and largest grassroots human rights organization. Since 1961, ordinary people across the world have chosen to take extraordinary action in defense of human rights for all.

https://www.amnestyusa.org/press-releases/amnesty-international-will-defend-human-rights-during-president-elect-trumps-second-term/

American Civil Liberties (ACLU)

The ACLU works to ensure that lesbian, gay, bisexual, transgender and queer people can live openly without discrimination and enjoy equal rights, personal autonomy, and freedom of expression and association.

A Martial Law Primer
The insurrection Act

In my opinion, martial law is a very real possibility during Donald Trump's presidency

We are looking at the birth of massive civil rights violations that can bring great violence to our nation.

What is Martial Law?
This is the actual law, which gives the President of the United States the power to declare martial law. Marial law can be declared. Temporarily or permanently, and states also have the power to declare Martial Law.

During Martial Law, citizens will experience:

- **Suspension of civil liberties**: The military can suspend civil liberties including freedom of speech, journalism, freedom of movement, and protection from unreasonable searches, and protests.
  - **Curfews**: Curfews can and probably will be implemented.
  - **Unlimited authority for military commanders**: Military commanders can make and enforce laws, arrest people, and mete out punishment based on military needs.
  - **Suspension of legal processes**: Civilian legal processes are suspended, and only military tribunals are used.

When people protest against these expected issues, will the president enact Martial Law to stop them?

- The mobilization of armed military used against protests

- Abortion bans that may become Federal law
- The high risk of Trump's agencies to make abortion medications illegal due to some "new" issue
- Giant surprise raids in Sanctuary cities, most always in Democratic states, conducted by the National Guard to forcibly remove undocumented immigrants, even from their children
- Dismantling of the Department of Education, which includes Civil Rights act to protect all students, plus censorship of major historic and current realities
- Rolling back LBGTQI rights of all kinds, which may include marriage, etc.
- Trans-students rights, and denied access to medicine they sorely need
- Retaliation of some kind against anyone Trump deems "from the deep state" or as his enemy because they are political opponents, etc.
- Fines or imprisonment for journalists who dared to write articles or books that Trump dislikes
- Racial violence and hate crimes

Dear Readers,

Thank you for reading this book and guide, which I hope helps you briefly understand some of the daunting issues facing us today, as we face an unthinkable, anti-human rights America.

I hope you will take nonviolent action, and that we will vote in mid-terms and in the next election in four years to choose Congress and the 48th president of these United States of America.

I am not optimistic about the next four years, but I am hopeful that we can work hard to keep our Democracy alive and protect those who are suffering from human rights violations here in the USA. We will lose some battles, I expect.

Perhaps in four years, millions of Americans who voted for Donald Trump will agree with us that the disruptive changes he brings to America do not work in our Democracy.

I hope and pray that the tragic political divide we face now may be healed in four years, by the crystal-clear realities of all the broken promises and crushed human rights laws that Project 2025 far-right leaders and the Trump administration are serving us now.

But what is we do spiral into some form of a fascist government? I have no answers for that, but as I write here in the birthplace of the United States of America, in Philadelphia, I can tell you that our Liberty Bell, which is the symbol of protest in our democracy, may be cracked and ready to survive. See you on the other sie,

Best,

Diane Lilli

How to Stop Project 2025

Watch List: Programs that may be cut by Elon Musk and Vivek Ramaswamy, heads of the new "Dept. of Efficiency."

The new Department of Efficiency, led by Elon Musk and Vivek Ramaswamy, will swing into gear after Inauguration Day on January 20. 2025. These are some of the vital programs that are threatened.

Housing Aid for Millions
The Quality Housing and Work Responsibility Act was passed in 1998, and offers federal housing, such as voucher programs and assistance to poverty-stricken citizens. The Act is under The Department of Housing and Urban Development.

Threat to Disabled Citizens
In Project 2025, which is greatly influencing incoming President Trump's polices and cabinet, there is a plan to limit federal agencies including rules that protect disability rights.

Veterans' health Care and Support
Veteran's hospital, nursing home and medical care are approved under Congress, under a 1996 law. The Department of Veterans Affairs (VA), which covers over 9 million Americans, may be in danger of being dismantled or hit with catastrophic cut.

The Affordable Care Act
The Affordable Care Act, passed into law in 2020 and called Obamacare, is in jeopardy. Millions of Americans rely upon this care and insurance program, that offers affordable plans to about 45 million people.

Head Start
Head Start supports over 800,000 children in U.S. schools who are from low-income families. Head start offers a robust preschool program, where children receive nutrition, health and the program supports that help them grow mentally, physically and socially.

Opioid and Drug Treatment
This 21st Century Cures Act of 2016 funds state grants for opioid addiction and drug treatments, plus medical trails and pharmaceutical research. The Act is part of the National Institutes of Heald and the FDA, which are also threatened at this time.

Beginning with the words "We the People," the U.S. Constitution is composed of the Preamble, seven articles, and 27 amendments. The first 10 amendments are known as the Bill of Rights. Please note: this is the original Constitution with all amendments, and some of the words are spelled differently than today.

The Constitution

Beginning with the words "We the People," the U.S. Constitution is composed of the Preamble, seven articles, and 27 amendments.

The first 10 amendments are known as the Bill of Rights.

The Constitution of the United States of America

The Preamble

We the People of the United States, in Order to form a more perfect Union, establish Justice, insure domestic Tranquility, provide for the common defense, promote the general Welfare, and secure the Blessings of Liberty to ourselves and our Posterity, do ordain and establish this Constitution for the United States of America.

Article I

Section 1

All legislative Powers herein granted shall be vested in a Congress of the United States, which shall consist of a Senate and House of Representatives.

Section 2

The House of Representatives shall be composed of Members chosen every second Year by the People of the several States, and the Electors in each State shall have the Qualifications requisite for Electors of the most numerous Branch of the State Legislature.

No Person shall be a Representative who shall not have attained to the Age of twenty five Years, and been seven Years a

Citizen of the United States, and who shall not, when elected, be an Inhabitant of that State in which he shall be chosen.

Representatives and direct Taxes shall be apportioned among the several States which may be included within this Union, according to their respective Numbers, which shall be determined by adding to the whole Number of free Persons, including those bound to Service for a Term of Years, and excluding Indians not taxed, three fifths of all other Persons. The actual Enumeration shall be made within three Years after the first Meeting of the Congress of the United States, and within every subsequent Term of ten Years, in such Manner as they shall by Law direct. The Number of Representatives shall not exceed one for every thirty Thousand, but each State shall have at Least one Representative; and until such enumeration shall be made, the State of New Hampshire shall be entitled to chuse three, Massachusetts eight, Rhode Island and Providence Plantations one, Connecticut five, New-York six, New Jersey four, Pennsylvania eight, Delaware one, Maryland six, Virginia ten, North Carolina five, South Carolina five, and Georgia three.

When vacancies happen in the Representation from any State, the Executive Authority thereof shall issue Writs of Election to fill such Vacancies.

The House of Representatives shall chuse their Speaker and other Officers; and shall have the sole Power of Impeachment.

Section 3

The Senate of the United States shall be composed of two Senators from each State, chosen by the Legislature thereof, for six Years; and each Senator shall have one Vote.

Immediately after they shall be assembled in Consequence of the first Election, they shall be divided as equally as may be into three Classes. The Seats of the Senators of the first Class shall be vacated at the Expiration of the second Year, of the second Class at the Expiration of the fourth Year, and of the third Class at the Expiration of the sixth Year, so that one third may be chosen every second Year; and if Vacancies happen by Resignation, or otherwise, during the Recess of the Legislature of any State, the Executive thereof may make temporary Appointments until the next Meeting of the Legislature, which shall then fill such Vacancies.

No Person shall be a Senator who shall not have attained to the Age of thirty Years, and been nine Years a Citizen of the United States, and who shall not, when elected, be an Inhabitant of that State for which he shall be chosen.

The Vice President of the United States shall be President of the Senate, but shall have no Vote, unless they be equally divided.

The Senate shall chuse their other Officers, and also a President pro tempore, in the Absence of the Vice President, or when he shall exercise the Office of President of the United States.

The Senate shall have the sole Power to try all Impeachments. When sitting for that Purpose, they shall be on Oath or Affirmation. When the President of the United States is tried, the Chief Justice shall preside: And no Person shall be convicted without the Concurrence of two thirds of the Members present.

Judgment in Cases of Impeachment shall not extend further than to removal from Office, and disqualification to hold and enjoy any Office of honor, Trust or Profit under the United States: but the Party convicted shall nevertheless be liable and subject to Indictment, Trial, Judgment and Punishment, according to Law.

Section 4

The Times, Places and Manner of holding Elections for Senators and Representatives, shall be prescribed in each State by the Legislature thereof; but the Congress may at any time by Law make or alter such Regulations, except as to the Places of chusing Senators.

The Congress shall assemble at least once in every Year, and such Meeting shall be on the first Monday in December, unless they shall by Law appoint a different Day.

Section 5

Each House shall be the Judge of the Elections, Returns and Qualifications of its own Members, and a Majority of each shall constitute a Quorum to do Business; but a smaller Number may adjourn from day to day, and may be authorized to compel the Attendance of absent Members, in such Manner, and under such Penalties as each House may provide.

Each House may determine the Rules of its Proceedings, punish its Members for disorderly Behaviour, and, with the Concurrence of two thirds, expel a Member.

Each House shall keep a Journal of its Proceedings, and from time to time publish the same, excepting such Parts as may in their Judgment require Secrecy; and the Yeas and Nays of the Members of either House on any question shall, at the Desire of one fifth of those Present, be entered on the Journal.

Neither House, during the Session of Congress, shall, without the Consent of the other, adjourn for more than three days, nor to any other Place than that in which the two Houses shall be sitting.

Section 6

The Senators and Representatives shall receive a Compensation for their Services, to be ascertained by Law, and paid out of the Treasury of the United States. They shall in all Cases, except Treason, Felony and Breach of the Peace, be privileged from Arrest during their Attendance at the Session of their respective Houses, and in going to and returning from the same; and for any Speech or Debate in either House, they shall not be questioned in any other Place.

No Senator or Representative shall, during the Time for which he was elected, be appointed to any civil Office under the Authority of the United States, which shall have been created, or the Emoluments whereof shall have been encreased during such time; and no Person holding any Office under the United States, shall be a Member of either House during his Continuance in Office.

Section 7

All Bills for raising Revenue shall originate in the House of Representatives; but the Senate may propose or concur with Amendments as on other Bills.

Every Bill which shall have passed the House of Representatives and the Senate, shall, before it become a Law, be presented to the President of the United States; If he approve he shall sign it, but if not he shall return it, with his Objections to that House in which it shall have originated, who shall enter the Objections at large on their Journal, and proceed to reconsider it. If after such Reconsideration two thirds of that House shall agree to pass the Bill, it shall be sent, together with the Objections, to the other House, by which it shall likewise be reconsidered, and if approved by two thirds of that House, it shall become a Law. But in all such Cases the Votes of both Houses shall be determined by yeas and Nays, and the Names of the Persons voting for and against the Bill shall be entered on the Journal of each House respectively. If any Bill shall not be returned by the President within ten Days (Sundays excepted) after it shall have been presented to him, the Same shall be a Law, in like Manner as if he had signed it, unless the Congress by their Adjournment prevent its Return, in which Case it shall not be a Law.

Every Order, Resolution, or Vote to which the Concurrence of the Senate and House of Representatives may be necessary (except on a question of Adjournment) shall be presented to the President of the United States; and before the Same shall take Effect, shall be approved by him, or being disapproved by him, shall be repassed by two thirds of the Senate and House of Representatives, according to the Rules and Limitations prescribed in the Case of a Bill.

Section 8

The Congress shall have Power To lay and collect Taxes, Duties, Imposts and Excises, to pay the Debts and provide for the common Defence and general Welfare of the United States; but all

Duties, Imposts and Excises shall be uniform throughout the United States;

To borrow Money on the credit of the United States;

To regulate Commerce with foreign Nations, and among the several States, and with the Indian Tribes;

To establish an uniform Rule of Naturalization, and uniform Laws on the subject of Bankruptcies throughout the United States;

To coin Money, regulate the Value thereof, and of foreign Coin, and fix the Standard of Weights and Measures;

To provide for the Punishment of counterfeiting the Securities and current Coin of the United States;

To establish Post Offices and post Roads;

To promote the Progress of Science and useful Arts, by securing for limited Times to Authors and Inventors the exclusive Right to their respective Writings and Discoveries;

To constitute Tribunals inferior to the supreme Court;

To define and punish Piracies and Felonies committed on the high Seas, and Offences against the Law of Nations;

To declare War, grant Letters of Marque and Reprisal, and make Rules concerning Captures on Land and Water;

To raise and support Armies, but no Appropriation of Money to that Use shall be for a longer Term than two Years;

To provide and maintain a Navy;

To make Rules for the Government and Regulation of the land and naval Forces;

To provide for calling forth the Militia to execute the Laws of the Union, suppress Insurrections and repel Invasions;

To provide for organizing, arming, and disciplining, the Militia, and for governing such Part of them as may be employed in the Service of the United States, reserving to the States respectively, the Appointment of the Officers, and the Authority of training the Militia according to the discipline prescribed by Congress;

To exercise exclusive Legislation in all Cases whatsoever, over such District (not exceeding ten Miles square) as may, by Cession of particular States, and the Acceptance of Congress, become the Seat of Government of the United States, and to exercise like Authority over all Places purchased by the Consent of the Legislature of the State in which the Same shall be, for the Erection of Forts, Magazines, Arsenals, dock-Yards, and other needful Buildings;–And

To make all Laws which shall be necessary and proper for carrying into Execution the foregoing Powers, and all other Powers vested by this Constitution in the Government of the United States, or in any Department or Officer thereof.

Section 9

The Migration or Importation of such Persons as any of the States now existing shall think proper to admit, shall not be prohibited by the Congress prior to the Year one thousand eight hundred and eight, but a Tax or duty may be imposed on such Importation, not exceeding ten dollars for each Person.

The Privilege of the Writ of Habeas Corpus shall not be suspended, unless when in Cases of Rebellion or Invasion the public Safety may require it.

No Bill of Attainder or ex post facto Law shall be passed.

No Capitation, or other direct, Tax shall be laid, unless in Proportion to the Census or enumeration herein before directed to be taken.

No Tax or Duty shall be laid on Articles exported from any State.

No Preference shall be given by any Regulation of Commerce or Revenue to the Ports of one State over those of another: nor shall Vessels bound to, or from, one State, be obliged to enter, clear, or pay Duties in another.

No Money shall be drawn from the Treasury, but in Consequence of Appropriations made by Law; and a regular Statement and Account of the Receipts and Expenditures of all public Money shall be published from time to time.

No Title of Nobility shall be granted by the United States: And no Person holding any Office of Profit or Trust under them, shall, without the Consent of the Congress, accept of any present, Emolument, Office, or Title, of any kind whatever, from any King, Prince, or foreign State.

Section 10

No State shall enter into any Treaty, Alliance, or Confederation; grant Letters of Marque and Reprisal; coin Money; emit Bills of Credit; make any Thing but gold and silver Coin a Tender in Payment of Debts; pass any Bill of Attainder, ex post facto Law, or Law impairing the Obligation of Contracts, or grant any Title of Nobility.

No State shall, without the Consent of the Congress, lay any Imposts or Duties on Imports or Exports, except what may be absolutely necessary for executing it's inspection Laws: and the net Produce of all Duties and Imposts, laid by any State on Imports or Exports, shall be for the Use of the Treasury of the United States; and all such Laws shall be subject to the Revision and Controul of the Congress.

No State shall, without the Consent of Congress, lay any Duty of Tonnage, keep Troops, or Ships of War in time of Peace, enter into any Agreement or Compact with another State, or with a foreign Power, or engage in War, unless actually invaded, or in such imminent Danger as will not admit of delay.

Article II

Section 1

The executive Power shall be vested in a President of the United States of America. He shall hold his Office during the Term of four Years, and, together with the Vice President, chosen for the same Term, be elected, as follows

Each State shall appoint, in such Manner as the Legislature thereof may direct, a Number of Electors, equal to the whole Number of Senators and Representatives to which the State may be entitled in the Congress: but no Senator or Representative, or

Person holding an Office of Trust or Profit under the United States, shall be appointed an Elector.

The Electors shall meet in their respective States, and vote by Ballot for two Persons, of whom one at least shall not be an Inhabitant of the same State with themselves. And they shall make a List of all the Persons voted for, and of the Number of Votes for each; which List they shall sign and certify, and transmit sealed to the Seat of the Government of the United States, directed to the President of the Senate. The President of the Senate shall, in the Presence of the Senate and House of Representatives, open all the Certificates, and the Votes shall then be counted. The Person having the greatest Number of Votes shall be the President, if such Number be a Majority of the whole Number of Electors appointed; and if there be more than one who have such Majority, and have an equal Number of Votes, then the House of Representatives shall immediately chuse by Ballot one of them for President; and if no Person have a Majority, then from the five highest on the List the said House shall in like Manner chuse the President. But in chusing the President, the Votes shall be taken by States, the Representation from each State having one Vote; A quorum for this Purpose shall consist of a Member or Members from two thirds of the States, and a Majority of all the States shall be necessary to a Choice. In every Case, after the Choice of the President, the Person having the greatest Number of Votes of the Electors shall be the Vice President. But if there should remain two or more who have equal Votes, the Senate shall chuse from them by Ballot the Vice President.

The Congress may determine the Time of chusing the Electors, and the Day on which they shall give their Votes; which Day shall be the same throughout the United States.

No Person except a natural born Citizen, or a Citizen of the United States, at the time of the Adoption of this Constitution, shall be eligible to the Office of President; neither shall any Person be eligible to that Office who shall not have attained to the Age of thirty five Years, and been fourteen Years a Resident within the United States.

In Case of the Removal of the President from Office, or of his Death, Resignation, or Inability to discharge the Powers and Duties of the said Office, the Same shall devolve on the Vice President, and the Congress may by law provide for the Case of Removal, Death, Resignation or Inability, both of the President and Vice President, declaring what Officer shall then act as President, and such Officer shall act accordingly, until the Disability be removed, or a President shall be elected.

The President shall, at stated Times, receive for his Services, a Compensation, which shall neither be encreased nor diminished during the Period for which he shall have been elected, and he shall not receive within that Period any other Emolument from the United States, or any of them.

Before he enter on the Execution of his Office, he shall take the following Oath or Affirmation:– I do solemnly swear (or affirm) that I will faithfully execute the Office of President of the United States, and will to the best of my Ability, preserve, protect and defend the Constitution of the United States.

Section 2

The President shall be Commander in Chief of the Army and Navy of the United States, and of the Militia of the several States, when called into the actual Service of the United States; he may require the Opinion, in writing, of the principal Officer in each of the executive Departments, upon any Subject relating to the Duties of their respective Offices, and he shall have Power to grant Reprieves and Pardons for Offences against the United States, except in Cases of Impeachment.

He shall have Power, by and with the Advice and Consent of the Senate, to make Treaties, provided two thirds of the Senators present concur; and he shall nominate, and by and with the Advice and Consent of the Senate, shall appoint Ambassadors, other public Ministers and Consuls, Judges of the supreme Court, and all other Officers of the United States, whose Appointments are not herein otherwise provided for, and which shall be established by Law: but the Congress may by Law vest the Appointment of such inferior Officers, as they think proper, in the President alone, in the Courts of Law, or in the Heads of Departments.

The President shall have Power to fill up all Vacancies that may happen during the Recess of the Senate, by granting Commissions which shall expire at the End of their next Session.

Section 3

He shall from time to time give to the Congress Information of the State of the Union, and recommend to their Consideration such Measures as he shall judge necessary and expedient; he may, on extraordinary Occasions, convene both Houses, or either of them, and in Case of Disagreement between them, with Respect to the Time of Adjournment, he may adjourn them to such Time as he shall think proper; he shall receive Ambassadors and other public Ministers; he shall take Care that the Laws be faithfully executed, and shall Commission all the Officers of the United States.

Section 4

The President, Vice President and all civil Officers of the United States, shall be removed from Office on Impeachment for, and Conviction of, Treason, Bribery, or other high Crimes and Misdemeanors.

Article III

Section 1

The judicial Power of the United States, shall be vested in one supreme Court, and in such inferior Courts as the Congress may from time to time ordain and establish. The Judges, both of the supreme and inferior Courts, shall hold their Offices during good Behaviour, and shall, at stated Times, receive for their Services, a Compensation, which shall not be diminished during their Continuance in Office.

Section 2

The judicial Power shall extend to all Cases, in Law and Equity, arising under this Constitution, the Laws of the United States, and Treaties made, or which shall be made, under their Authority;—to all Cases affecting Ambassadors, other public Ministers and Consuls;—to all Cases of admiralty and maritime Jurisdiction;—to Controversies to which the United States shall be a Party;—to Controversies between two or more States;—between a State and Citizens of another State,—between Citizens of different States,—between Citizens of the same State claiming Lands under Grants of different States, and between a State, or the Citizens thereof, and foreign States, Citizens or Subjects.

In all Cases affecting Ambassadors, other public Ministers and Consuls, and those in which a State shall be Party, the supreme Court shall have original Jurisdiction. In all the other Cases before mentioned, the supreme Court shall have appellate Jurisdiction, both as to Law and Fact, with such Exceptions, and under such Regulations as the Congress shall make.

The Trial of all Crimes, except in Cases of Impeachment, shall be by Jury; and such Trial shall be held in the State where the said Crimes shall have been committed; but when not committed within any State, the Trial shall be at such Place or Places as the Congress may by Law have directed.

Section 3

Treason against the United States, shall consist only in levying War against them, or in adhering to their Enemies, giving them Aid and Comfort. No Person shall be convicted of Treason unless on the Testimony of two Witnesses to the same overt Act, or on Confession in open Court.

The Congress shall have Power to declare the Punishment of Treason, but no Attainder of Treason shall work Corruption of Blood, or Forfeiture except during the Life of the Person attainted.

Article IV

Section 1

Full Faith and Credit shall be given in each State to the public Acts, Records, and judicial Proceedings of every other State. And the Congress may by general Laws prescribe the Manner in which such Acts, Records and Proceedings shall be proved, and the Effect thereof.

Section 2

The Citizens of each State shall be entitled to all Privileges and Immunities of Citizens in the several States.

A Person charged in any State with Treason, Felony, or other Crime, who shall flee from Justice, and be found in another State, shall on Demand of the executive Authority of the State from which he fled, be delivered up, to be removed to the State having Jurisdiction of the Crime.

No Person held to Service or Labour in one State, under the Laws thereof, escaping into another, shall, in Consequence of any Law or Regulation therein, be discharged from such Service or Labour, but shall be delivered up on Claim of the Party to whom such Service or Labour may be due.

Section 3

New States may be admitted by the Congress into this Union; but no new State shall be formed or erected within the Jurisdiction of any other State; nor any State be formed by the Junction of two or more States, or Parts of States, without the Consent of the Legislatures of the States concerned as well as of the Congress.

The Congress shall have Power to dispose of and make all needful Rules and Regulations respecting the Territory or other Property belonging to the United States; and nothing in this Constitution shall be so construed as to Prejudice any Claims of the United States, or of any particular State.

Section 4

The United States shall guarantee to every State in this Union a Republican Form of Government, and shall protect each of them against Invasion; and on Application of the Legislature, or of the

Executive (when the Legislature cannot be convened) against domestic Violence.

Article V

The Congress, whenever two thirds of both Houses shall deem it necessary, shall propose Amendments to this Constitution, or, on the Application of the Legislatures of two thirds of the several States, shall call a Convention for proposing Amendments, which, in either Case, shall be valid to all Intents and Purposes, as Part of this Constitution, when ratified by the Legislatures of three fourths of the several States, or by Conventions in three fourths thereof, as the one or the other Mode of Ratification may be proposed by the Congress; Provided that no Amendment which may be made prior to the Year One thousand eight hundred and eight shall in any Manner affect the first and fourth Clauses in the Ninth Section of the first Article; and that no State, without its Consent, shall be deprived of its equal Suffrage in the Senate.

Article VI

All Debts contracted and Engagements entered into, before the Adoption of this Constitution, shall be as valid against the United States under this Constitution, as under the Confederation.

This Constitution, and the Laws of the United States which shall be made in Pursuance thereof; and all Treaties made, or which shall be made, under the Authority of the United States, shall be the supreme Law of the Land; and the Judges in every State shall be bound thereby, any Thing in the Constitution or Laws of any State to the Contrary notwithstanding.

The Senators and Representatives before mentioned, and the Members of the several State Legislatures, and all executive and judicial Officers, both of the United States and of the several States, shall be bound by Oath or Affirmation, to support this Constitution; but no religious Test shall ever be required as a Qualification to any Office or public Trust under the United States.

Article VII

The Ratification of the Conventions of nine States, shall be sufficient for the Establishment of this Constitution between the States so ratifying the Same.

First Amendment

Congress shall make no law respecting an establishment of religion, or prohibiting the free exercise thereof; or abridging the freedom of speech, or of the press; or the right of the people peaceably to assemble, and to petition the Government for a redress of grievances.

Second Amendment

A well regulated Militia, being necessary to the security of a free State, the right of the people to keep and bear Arms, shall not be infringed.

Third Amendment

No Soldier shall, in time of peace be quartered in any house, without the consent of the Owner, nor in time of war, but in a manner to be prescribed by law.

Fourth Amendment

The right of the people to be secure in their persons, houses, papers, and effects, against unreasonable searches and seizures, shall not be violated, and no Warrants shall issue, but upon probable cause, supported by Oath or affirmation, and particularly describing the place to be searched, and the persons or things to be seized.

Fifth Amendment

No person shall be held to answer for a capital, or otherwise infamous crime, unless on a presentment or indictment of a Grand Jury, except in cases arising in the land or naval forces, or in the Militia, when in actual service in time of War or public danger; nor shall any person be subject for the same offence to be twice put in jeopardy of life or limb; nor shall be compelled in any criminal case to be a witness against himself, nor be deprived of life, liberty, or property, without due process of law; nor shall private property be taken for public use, without just compensation.

Sixth Amendment

In all criminal prosecutions, the accused shall enjoy the right to a speedy and public trial, by an impartial jury of the State and district wherein the crime shall have been committed, which district shall have been previously ascertained by law, and to be informed of the nature and cause of the accusation; to be confronted with the witnesses against him; to have compulsory process for obtaining witnesses in his favor, and to have the Assistance of Counsel for his defence.

Seventh Amendment

In Suits at common law, where the value in controversy shall exceed twenty dollars, the right of trial by jury shall be preserved, and no fact tried by a jury, shall be otherwise re-examined in any Court of the United States, than according to the rules of the common law.

Eighth Amendment

Excessive bail shall not be required, nor excessive fines imposed, nor cruel and unusual punishments inflicted.

Ninth Amendment

The enumeration in the Constitution, of certain rights, shall not be construed to deny or disparage others retained by the people.

Tenth Amendment

The powers not delegated to the United States by the Constitution, nor prohibited by it to the States, are reserved to the States respectively, or to the people.

Eleventh Amendment

The Judicial power of the United States shall not be construed to extend to any suit in law or equity, commenced or prosecuted against one of the United States by Citizens of another State, or by Citizens or Subjects of any Foreign State.

Twelfth Amendment

The Electors shall meet in their respective states and vote by ballot for President and Vice-President, one of whom, at least, shall not be an inhabitant of the same state with themselves; they shall name in their ballots the person voted for as President, and in distinct ballots the person voted for as Vice-President, and they shall make distinct lists of all persons voted for as President, and of all persons voted for as Vice-President, and of the number of votes for each, which lists they shall sign and certify, and transmit sealed to the seat of the government of the United States, directed to the President of the Senate;–the President of the Senate shall, in the presence of the Senate and House of Representatives, open all the certificates and the votes shall then be counted;–The person having the greatest number of votes for President, shall be the President, if such number be a majority of the whole number of Electors appointed; and if no person have such majority, then from the persons having the highest numbers not exceeding three on the list of those voted for as President, the House of Representatives shall choose immediately, by ballot, the President. But in choosing the President, the votes shall be taken by states, the representation from each state having one vote; a quorum for this purpose shall consist of a member or members from two-thirds of the states, and a majority of all the states shall be necessary to a choice. [And if the House of Representatives shall not choose a President whenever the right of choice shall devolve upon them, before the fourth day of March next following, then the Vice-President shall act as President, as in case of the death or other constitutional disability of the President.–]The person having the greatest number of votes as Vice-President, shall be the Vice-President, if such number be a majority of the whole number of Electors appointed, and if no person have a majority, then from the two highest numbers on the list, the Senate shall choose the Vice-President; a quorum for the purpose shall consist of two-thirds of the whole number of Senators, and a majority of the whole number shall be necessary to a choice. But no person constitutionally ineligible to the office of President shall be eligible to that of Vice-President of the United States.

Thirteenth Amendment

Section 1

Neither slavery nor involuntary servitude, except as a punishment for crime whereof the party shall have been duly convicted, shall exist within the United States, or any place subject to their jurisdiction.

Section 2

Congress shall have power to enforce this article by appropriate legislation.

Fourteenth Amendment

Section 1

All persons born or naturalized in the United States, and subject to the jurisdiction thereof, are citizens of the United States and of the State wherein they reside. No State shall make or enforce any law which shall abridge the privileges or immunities of citizens of the United States; nor shall any State deprive any person of life, liberty, or property, without due process of law; nor deny to any person within its jurisdiction the equal protection of the laws.

Section 2

Representatives shall be apportioned among the several States according to their respective numbers, counting the whole number of persons in each State, excluding Indians not taxed. But when the right to vote at any election for the choice of electors for President and Vice-President of the United States, Representatives in Congress, the Executive and Judicial officers of a State, or the members of the Legislature thereof, is denied to any of the male inhabitants of such State, being twenty-one years of age, and citizens of the United States, or in any way abridged, except for participation in rebellion, or other crime, the basis of representation therein shall be reduced in the proportion which the number of such male citizens shall bear to the whole number of male citizens twenty-one years of age in such State.

Section 3

No person shall be a Senator or Representative in Congress, or elector of President and Vice-President, or hold any office, civil or military, under the United States, or under any State, who, having previously taken an oath, as a member of Congress, or as an officer of the United States, or as a member of any State legislature, or as an executive or judicial officer of any State, to support the Constitution of the United States, shall have engaged in insurrection or rebellion against the same, or given aid or comfort to the enemies thereof. But Congress may by a vote of two-thirds of each House, remove such disability.

Section 4

The validity of the public debt of the United States, authorized by law, including debts incurred for payment of pensions and bounties for services in suppressing insurrection or rebellion, shall not be questioned. But neither the United States nor any State shall assume or pay any debt or obligation incurred in aid of insurrection or rebellion against the United States, or any claim for the loss or emancipation of any slave; but all such debts, obligations and claims shall be held illegal and void.

Section 5

The Congress shall have power to enforce, by appropriate legislation, the provisions of this article.

Fifteenth Amendment

Section 1

The right of citizens of the United States to vote shall not be denied or abridged by the United States or by any State on account of race, color, or previous condition of servitude–

Section 2

The Congress shall have power to enforce this article by appropriate legislation.

Sixteenth Amendment

Sixteenth Amendment Explained

The Congress shall have power to lay and collect taxes on incomes, from whatever source derived, without apportionment among the several States, and without regard to any census or enumeration.

Seventeenth Amendment

Seventeenth Amendment Explained

The Senate of the United States shall be composed of two Senators from each State, elected by the people thereof, for six years; and each Senator shall have one vote. The electors in each State shall have the qualifications requisite for electors of the most numerous branch of the State legislatures.

When vacancies happen in the representation of any State in the Senate, the executive authority of such State shall issue writs of election to fill such vacancies: Provided, That the legislature of any State may empower the executive thereof to make temporary appointments until the people fill the vacancies by election as the legislature may direct.

This amendment shall not be so construed as to affect the election or term of any Senator chosen before it becomes valid as part of the Constitution.

Eighteenth Amendment

After one year from the ratification of this article the manufacture, sale, or transportation of intoxicating liquors within, the importation thereof into, or the exportation thereof from the United States and all territory subject to the jurisdiction thereof for beverage purposes is hereby prohibited.

The Congress and the several States shall have concurrent power to enforce this article by appropriate legislation.

This article shall be inoperative unless it shall have been ratified as an amendment to the Constitution by the legislatures of the several States, as provided in the Constitution, within seven years from the date of the submission hereof to the States by the Congress.

Nineteenth Amendment

The right of citizens of the United States to vote shall not be denied or abridged by the United States or by any State on account of sex.

Congress shall have power to enforce this article by appropriate legislation.

Twentieth Amendment

Section 1

The terms of the President and the Vice President shall end at noon on the 20th day of January, and the terms of Senators and Representatives at noon on the 3d day of January, of the years in which such terms would have ended if this article had not been ratified; and the terms of their successors shall then begin.

Section 2

The Congress shall assemble at least once in every year, and such meeting shall begin at noon on the 3d day of January, unless they shall by law appoint a different day.

Section 3

If, at the time fixed for the beginning of the term of the President, the President elect shall have died, the Vice President elect shall become President. If a President shall not have been chosen before the time fixed for the beginning of his term, or if the President elect shall have failed to qualify, then the Vice President elect shall act as President until a President shall have qualified; and the Congress may by law provide for the case wherein neither a President elect nor a Vice President elect shall have qualified, declaring who shall then act as President, or the manner in which one who is to act shall be selected, and such person shall act accordingly until a President or Vice President shall have qualified.

Section 4

The Congress may by law provide for the case of the death of any of the persons from whom the House of Representatives may choose a President whenever the right of choice shall have devolved upon them, and for the case of the death of any of the persons from whom the Senate may choose a Vice President whenever the right of choice shall have devolved upon them.

Section 5

Sections 1 and 2 shall take effect on the 15th day of October following the ratification of this article.

Section 6

This article shall be inoperative unless it shall have been ratified as an amendment to the Constitution by the legislatures of three-fourths of the several States within seven years from the date of its submission.

Twenty-First Amendment

Section 1

The eighteenth article of amendment to the Constitution of the United States is hereby repealed.

Section 2

The transportation or importation into any State, Territory, or possession of the United States for delivery or use therein of intoxicating liquors, in violation of the laws thereof, is hereby prohibited.

Section 3

This article shall be inoperative unless it shall have been ratified as an amendment to the Constitution by conventions in the several States, as provided in the Constitution, within seven years from the date of the submission hereof to the States by the Congress.

Twenty-Second Amendment

Section 1

No person shall be elected to the office of the President more than twice, and no person who has held the office of President, or acted as President, for more than two years of a term to which some other person was elected President shall be elected to the office of the President more than once. But this Article shall not apply to any person holding the office of President when this Article was proposed by the Congress, and shall not prevent any person who may be holding the office of President, or acting as President, during the term within which this Article becomes operative from holding the office of President or acting as President during the remainder of such term.

Section 2

This article shall be inoperative unless it shall have been ratified as an amendment to the Constitution by the legislatures of three-fourths of the several States within seven years from the date of its submission to the States by the Congress.

Twenty-Third Amendment

Section 1

The District constituting the seat of Government of the United States shall appoint in such manner as the Congress may direct:

A number of electors of President and Vice President equal to the whole number of Senators and Representatives in Congress to which the District would be entitled if it were a State, but in no event more than the least populous State; they shall be in addition to those appointed by the States, but they shall be considered, for the purposes of the election of President and Vice President, to be electors appointed by a State; and they shall meet in the District and perform such duties as provided by the twelfth article of amendment.

Section 2

The Congress shall have power to enforce this article by appropriate legislation.

Twenty-Fourth Amendment

Section 1

The right of citizens of the United States to vote in any primary or other election for President or Vice President, for electors for President or Vice President, or for Senator or Representative in Congress, shall not be denied or abridged by the United States or any State by reason of failure to pay any poll tax or other tax.

Section 2

The Congress shall have power to enforce this article by appropriate legislation.

Twenty-Fifth Amendment

Section 1

In case of the removal of the President from office or of his death or resignation, the Vice President shall become President.

Section 2

Whenever there is a vacancy in the office of the Vice President, the President shall nominate a Vice President who shall take office upon confirmation by a majority vote of both Houses of Congress.

Section 3

Whenever the President transmits to the President pro tempore of the Senate and the Speaker of the House of Representatives his written declaration that he is unable to discharge the powers and duties of his office, and until he transmits to them a written declaration to the contrary, such powers and duties shall be discharged by the Vice President as Acting President.

Section 4

Whenever the Vice President and a majority of either the principal officers of the executive departments or of such other body as Congress may by law provide, transmit to the President pro tempore of the Senate and the Speaker of the House of Representatives their written declaration that the President is unable to discharge the powers and duties of his office, the Vice President shall immediately assume the powers and duties of the office as Acting President.

Thereafter, when the President transmits to the President pro tempore of the Senate and the Speaker of the House of Representatives his written declaration that no inability exists, he shall resume the powers and duties of his office unless the Vice President and a majority of either the principal officers of the executive department or of such other body as Congress may by law provide, transmit within four days to the President pro tempore of the Senate and the Speaker of the House of Representatives their written declaration that the President is unable to discharge the powers and duties of his office. Thereupon Congress shall decide the issue, assembling within forty-eight hours for that purpose if not in session. If the Congress, within twenty-one days after receipt of the latter written declaration, or, if Congress is not in session, within twenty-one days after Congress is required to assemble, determines by two-thirds vote of both Houses that the President is unable to discharge the powers and duties of his office, the Vice President shall continue to discharge the same as Acting President; otherwise, the President shall resume the powers and duties of his office.

Twenty-Sixth Amendment

Section 1

The right of citizens of the United States, who are eighteen years of age or older, to vote shall not be denied or abridged by the United States or by any State on account of age.

Section 2

The Congress shall have power to enforce this article by appropriate legislation.

Twenty-Seventh Amendment

Twenty-Seventh Amendment Explained

No law, varying the compensation for the services of the Senators and Representatives, shall take effect, until an election of Representatives shall have intervened.

www.ingramcontent.com/pod-product-compliance
Lightning Source LLC
LaVergne TN
LVHW092058060526
838201LV00047B/1458